What a Modern Catholic Believes About
MYSTICISM

by Robert Nowell

the thomas more press
chicago · illinois

CONTENTS

Except where noted, biblical quotations are taken from the *Jerusalem Bible*, Doubleday & Company, Garden City, New York.

DS: Denziger-Schönmetzer, *Enchiridion Symbolorum, Definitionum et Declarationum*, 33rd edition, Herder & Herder, New York, 1965.

Chapter One

IS MYSTICISM NECESSARY?

For a Christian living in the latter half of the twentieth century, mysticism automatically raises a number of difficulties. Particularly is this so if he or she happens to be a Catholic. Some things apparently implied by mysticism seem difficult, if not impossible, to reconcile with the insights into its own nature rediscovered by the Church at Vatican II. Mysticism seems to imply an other-worldly approach that is hard to square with the this-worldly character of Christianity. It suggests too sharp a distinction between natural and supernatural, with an overemphasis on the latter, in contrast to the recognition that nature and grace are inextricably intertwined and that any abstract distinction between the two runs the risk of distortion if pushed beyond a certain fairly narrow limit. It carries overtones of individualism and élitism at a time when the Church has realized anew that it is a community, the people of God, and the message it has been entrusted with is for all men, not for a small élite. It runs counter to the whole temper and outlook that over the past four hundred years has increasingly marked the world we live in: what may be termed the scientific attitude that values what is precise, what is rational, what can be measured, what is tangible, what is predictable—and this at a time when an increasing effort is being made not to present the Gospel as something totally detached from any human context but to interpret it in the terms of the world we live in here and now, and the way in which we perceive this world.

Yet the last quarter of a century in particular has seen a remarkable resurgence of interest in mysticism. Inside and outside the Church, more and more people are finding in the practice of meditation the essential still center around which their lives can revolve. We may find the spectacle of the middle-aged executive practising meditation as incongruous as Eric Gill found the spectacle of the Catholic bank-clerk or stockbroker,[1] but at the very least it represents a recognition of a need, a reaching-out for something other. There is the attraction of mysticism in its various Eastern, non-Christian forms, as developed by Buddhism or Hinduism or the Chinese philosophy of the Tao. No doubt there is in all this an element of fashionableness: To take an interest in Zen, or to sit at the feet of some guru (and pay handsomely for the privilege), becomes the "in" thing to do. No doubt, too, much of the attraction of Eastern mysticism lies precisely in the fact that it is non-Christian and can thus appeal to those who seem to have put off Christianity for life through childhood encounter with its less attractive forms of institutional expression or who regard Christianity as somehow unworthy of serious attention. But, again, there is an element here of reaching out for something that, for whatever reason, does not appear to be offered by the Churches.

And within the Church there has developed a renewed interest in prayer, meditation, contemplation and mysticism. Prayer-groups have sprung up among Catholics who ten or twenty years ago would have regarded prayer meetings as an embarrassing Evangelical phenomenon they were fortunately saved from through membership in the one true Church. Books on prayer and ways of prayer enjoy a ready sale. The writings of the great Christian mystics of the Middle Ages and the sixteenth century have found a new and receptive audience; it seems significant that, for example, virtually the whole corpus of the English medieval school of mysticism should now be available in paperback.

Then there is the charismatic renewal. What in this century began as a movement on the fringes of Protestantism has invaded the mainstream Churches. Sober and middle-of-the-road Catholics, Anglicans, Lutherans, Methodists, and Presbyterians have experienced for themselves such charismatic phenomena as speaking in tongues and other unusual signs of the presence of the Holy Spirit. This is not, strictly speaking, mysticism, but it is closely connected with it.

In the charismatic movement the emphasis is on direct experience of the immediate presence and impact of the Holy Spirit at work in the individual or the community, as opposed to the normal way in which we are aware of the Holy Spirit at work (when it is a question of interpreting a complex of events for which a purely human explanation exists—the achievements of Vatican II provide a good example—as evidence that the Holy Spirit is indeed among us).

Finally, there are wilder manifestations to be taken into consideration. Psychedelic drugs such as LSD may no longer have the same attraction as they used to possess, no doubt because everyone is more aware of the psychological and physiological risks that may be involved. But they offered and offer an apparent short-cut to experiences that for the mystic lie at the end of a long and hard road. It could well be that the short-cut is a delusion, that what is experienced by someone under the influence of mescalin or LSD is totally other than what is experienced by the mystic in infused contemplative prayer. For those of us who are neither mystics nor takers of psychedelic drugs there is no way of telling, beyond the improbable experiment of persuading a full-blown mystic to take mescalin or LSD and comparing his experiences under the influence of that drug with his experiences of contemplation. While other considerations tend to rule out any equivalence, because of an understandable distrust of short-cuts— "The gate is wide and the way is easy that leads to destruction" (Matt. 7:13)—and a suspicion that only what is achieved by struggle and labor is of value, there is at the same time the experience undergone by

Aldous Huxley in May, 1953, when, under the influence of four-tenths of a gram of mescalin, flowers in a vase were "a transience that was yet eternal life, a perpetual perishing that was at the same time pure Being, a bundle of minute, unique particulars in which, by some unspeakable and yet self-evident paradox, was to be seen the divine source of all existence." We are reminded of Thomas Traherne seeing the corn as orient and immortal wheat. And Huxley summed up his perception by saying: "The Beatific Vision, Sat Chit Ananda, Being-Awareness-Bliss—for the first time I understood, not on the verbal level, not by inchoate hints or at a distance, but precisely and completely what those prodigious syllables referred to."[2]

Huxley's plea for the universal availability of drug-induced enlightenment may have fallen on increasingly deaf ears, and Timothy Leary, the high priest of the drug culture, may have announced his conversion from it. But left behind by the psychedelic movement is what can fairly be described as a hunger for mystical experience that was mixed with a number of other and less worthy motives to give rise to it.

All these movements and tendencies add up to the kind of thing that Vatican II labeled the signs of the times. If, as Christians, we believe that God is at work in human history, then we cannot confine this activity either to a period now safely past, culminating in the life, death and resurrection of Jesus Christ, or within the confines of the visible Church. If we believe the

Church is a pilgrim Church, we have to recognize that at times it finds it hard to discern which road its pilgrimage should take. And at times that occur all too frequently, the Church becomes bogged down in the past. It becomes incapable of preaching the Gospel in a way that speaks directly to the needs and wants of men and women of that time and instead addresses itself to the needs and wants of their great-grandparents. It becomes incapable of leading mankind forward into the future that God is preparing for it.

On these occasions the Church has to be reminded from outside, and sometimes forcibly reminded, why it is here and what it is that it is meant to be preaching. If some aspect of what the Gospel is about is neglected within the Church, it is taken up outside the Church—but against the Church and against what the Church claims to stand for. An example is the Marxist protest against economic bondage. There were, of course, Christians who tried on an individual basis to alleviate the appalling miseries and injustices associated with the industrial revolution. But to question the necessity of the injustices built into the structures of capitalism, to suggest that mankind was capable and worthy of something better, was to subvert the foundations of the social order, and it was left to Marx and Engels to make the prophetic denunciation that was needed—in terms that inevitably attacked the Church as the provider of supernatural sanction for maintaining social and economic ills. Since then the Church has learnt that social justice is very much part of what the Gospel is all about. But meanwhile, the realization that people are not there to be exploited, that their work should be a means of liberation and not of servitude, has developed outside and against the Church, with the result not only that many of those most sensitive to the needs of their neighbor have become as it were inoculated against Christianity but also that new forms of tyranny and of the denial of human rights have sprung up and taken institutional shape, particularly in the Soviet Union and Eastern Europe.

Nor does the Church's failure to read the signs of the times always have such dramatic results. If it fails to take into account some new way in which the reality of the world around it is being interpreted and rejects the possibility of interpreting in these new categories the message with which it has been entrusted, the result may merely be a loss of credibility. If Christians are slow and reluctant to recognize that, for example, the development of psychoanalysis by Freud and his disciples is relevant to the liberation of man that is at the heart of the promise of salvation, or that techniques of scholarship and textual criticisms make it no longer possible to assert the Mosaic authorship of the Pentateuch, the literal historical sense of the first three chapters of Genesis, or the authenticity of the Johannine comma, as the Pontifical Biblical Commission and the Holy Office were doing around the turn of the century (cf. DS 3394, 3514, and 3681-2), then a totally unnecessary obstacle to faith is raised in the minds of those who cannot honestly do other than accept such new insights. And the impression is given that the Church's main concern is not truth but the defense of its past mistakes.

Mysticism, then, is something that Christians both individually and as a community need to take seriously. They need to see whether the renewed interest in mysticism both inside and outside the Church means that the Church is neglecting to place sufficient emphasis on one aspect of its many-faceted message, that it is running the risk of failing to maintain that balance of emphases in which orthodoxy lies. This may seem an unnecessarily grudging approach to what at first sight seems an authentic part of Christian experience and one that has continually been present in the Church's life, however rare and exceptional an occurrence it may be. But there are many Christians whose sincerity cannot be disputed but for whom mysticism seems totally antipathetic. Much of the sundering quality of that great dispute between Bossuet and Fénelon which led eventually to the latter's condemnation seems to have had its roots in the former's inability to sympathize with any mystic, including those whose orthodoxy had been established by canonization.[3] And in our own century a theologian of the stature of the Protestant Karl Barth shows the greatest possible suspicion of mysticism on account of the threat it seems to offer to his insistence on the otherness of

God, the gulf between God and man, the uniqueness of revelation, and the fact that Jesus Christ is the "one mediator between God and men" (1 Tim. 2:5). Those who regard mysticism as at best marginally Christian have also to be taken seriously.

First, though, it would be as well to try to define what it is we are talking about. By mysticism I understand the direct apprehension in this life of God as he is—a kind of foretaste of the beatific vision. Normally, as far as an outsider can judge, it is something that occurs only after a lengthy period of preparation and progressive purification of the mystic's mental activity. What is not involved includes what can loosely be termed mystical phenomena—visions, trances, various phenomena that today would be classified under the heading of ESP or extra-sensory perception such as levitation or apparently being able to read someone else's mind, as well as the manifestations associated with the charismatic movement. These, as mystical writers such as St John of the Cross make abundantly clear, are at best stages on the road, and comparatively early stages at that. Nor shall I be concerned with the vague mystical feelings any of us is liable to experience from time to time—the kind of feelings that can be aroused, say, by a cathedral like Chartres, by listening to music, by being struck by the staggering beauty of woods or mountains. Wordsworth may have experienced intimations of immortality, and Marvell may have felt a garden as:

13

>   Annihilating all that's made
>   To a green Thought in a green Shade.

But such moments are at best pointers towards mysticism, indications that perhaps we too should try to cultivate the spirit of contemplation. They are not to be confused with mysticism itself.

Chapter Two

IS MYSTICISM CHRISTIAN?

At first glance, when contrasted with, say, Buddhism or Hinduism, Christianity can seem profoundly and fundamentally this-worldly and anti-mystical. To the outsider, the aim of Buddhism appears to be to break free from the shackles of this earthly life and to achieve that union with the underlying reality of all things that is the summit of mystical experience. The goal is the attainment of enlightenment *within* this life. Admittedly, enlightenment comes as the culmination of this life. But it is a culmination that seems to find its place this side of the barrier of death rather than beyond it. And reaching this culmination is presented as a process of stripping oneself of all attachment to the world of sense and sense-perception.

In sharp contrast, Christianity affirms the value and validity of this world of sense and sense-perception, of the here and now in which we live our lives. It makes the staggering claim that "God so loved the world that he gave his only Son," that God sent his Son into the world "not to condemn the world, but that the world might be saved through him" (John 3:16-17). The incarnation thus reaffirms and expands to the highest possible value the insights recorded in the first chapters of Genesis, that God created the world and "saw that it was good" (Gen. 1:4, 10, 12, 18, 21, 25, 31) and that he "created man in his own image" (Gen. 1:27). Right from the start there is the assertion of a profound and unshakeable identity between God and man alongside the assertion of a deep gulf between them: "What is man that thou art mindful of him, and the son of man that thou dost care for him?" asked the psalmist, and went on to answer his questions (Ps. 8:4-6): "Yet thou has made him little less than God, and dost crown him with glory and honour. Thou has given him dominion over the works of thy hands; thou hast put all things under his feet."

And God did not merely create man and the world as something good in itself and leave it at that. The message of the incarnation is the intensity of God's love for his creation. God so loved the world that he "emptied himself, taking the form of a slave, being born in the likeness of men" (Phil. 2:7). Our redemption was achieved at the cost of God becoming man and sharing the utmost degradation and suffering that mankind can inflict on itself: "And being found in human form he humbled himself and became obedient unto death, even death on a cross" (Phil. 2:8). Salvation is offered not in terms of rejecting human life but in terms of making it holy and purifying it. And the message of salvation is proclaimed here and now, in the midst of and in the terms of all our human comings and goings. To illustrate the relationship between Christ and his Church Paul developed his great analogy of marriage—and marriage encapsulates earthly human nature from the blind instincts of sex and reproduction to the most profound unselfishness love is capable of.

The message of salvation is proclaimed not as a turning away from the world but as a becoming even more deeply involved in the world. It is presented in very down-to-earth and concrete terms. The good news Jesus came to preach to the poor is release for captives, sight for the blind, freedom for those who are oppressed (Luke 4:18-19 quoting Isaiah 61:1-2). What it entails is brought out strongly in Jesus' answer to the scribe who asked which was the greatest commandment (Mark 12:28-31) or alternatively to the lawyer who asked what he should do to inherit eternal life (Luke 10:25-28): Love God and love your neighbor. It is startling the way in which Jesus ignores the terms in which the question is put to him and refuses to say either "love God" or "love your neighbor". Instead the two commandments are indissolubly linked and presented as the single great commandment, the fundamental obligation on man if he is to be truly human. We must not be tempted either to concentrate on God so much that we neglect our fellow-men or to concentrate on man so much, to become so bogged down in purely human categories, that we neglect God. Instead, to love God we must learn to love other people, to respond to their needs rather than exploiting them, and to learn to love other people we must learn to love God. We cannot abstract one from the other.

The lesson that we can only be said to love God if we genuinely love our neighbor is driven home in Jesus' discourse on the last judgment (Matt. 25:31-46). It is those who have been able to respond openly and automatically to their neighbors' needs who are welcomed into the kingdom—apparently even if they have not been able to recognize that in loving their neighbor they are loving God (vv. 37-40). The lesson is underlined in the first epistle of John. Loving each other is how we must respond to the love God has shown us in Jesus Christ: "If God so loved us, we also ought to love one another. No man has ever seen God; if we love one another, God abides in us and his love is perfected in us" (1 John 4:11-12). And the epistle of James makes the same point: "Faith by itself, if it has no works, is dead" (James 2:17). Love of God is shown in love of man.

Loving other people, then, is what Christianity is all about. But it is by no means all that Christianity is about. Nor can Christianity be reduced simply to terms of human relationships. It is very much concerned with this world, but at the same time it transcends this world. What we are offered is life—the life of the kingdom that has its roots in but transcends this world in a way we can as yet hardly understand. The promise of the resurrection is the promise that, in the words of the preface for the dead, our life will be not destroyed but changed. The radically new perspective of Christianity is that death is no longer the end, destroying all our aspirations and achievements and draining them of value and meaning, but marks a total transformation into life in its as yet unimaginable fullness. In other words, Christianity may be concerned with an "other world," but it is an "other world" that is not totally other. There is an element of essential continuity between this world and the next—something that, for example, is brought out by the doctrine of the communion of saints, the idea that all believers, those who have died and those who are still living, are indissolubly united in the Lord Jesus.

This essential continuity means that the kingdom of heaven is at hand and at the same time has come upon us. It is something that is not yet, it awaits its consummation in the second coming, but at the same time it is being built up here and now and signs of its presence are continually breaking in on us. Wherever evil is decisively overcome, wherever men and women are able genuinely to love one another instead of exploiting each other and are able to become reconciled with each other, there the kingdom of God is being built up. It is in this sense that the Church, the community of those who believe in the Lord Jesus, can be identified with the kingdom. It is not the kingdom itself, for that is something the Church too is still awaiting, is on pilgrimage towards; but it is the sign of the kingdom, the manifestation that the kingdom is at hand and has come upon us.

It is chiefly in this sense that we need to understand

the signs and wonders that accompanied and accompany the preaching of the Gospel. They are not, for the most part, events that are otherwise totally inexplicable except on the assumption that God is here intervening directly and miraculously in his creation. Rather is it a question of interpreting otherwise natural and explicable events as evidence of God working to save his people. It is in this way that the phrase "signs and wonders" is used in the Old Testament, above all in Deuteronomy, to describe the events leading up to the Exodus from Egypt. In their being led out of Egypt the people of Israel recognized a revolutionary turning-point in their history which they saw as proof of God's love and care for his people. No doubt the Egyptians preferred a different interpretation. And many of the signs and wonders that accompanied the preaching of the Gospel seem to be open to this ambiguity of interpretation. One immediate reaction to the apostles' proclamation of the mighty works of God after they had been filled with the Holy Spirit was that they were drunk—in sharp contrast to Peter's interpretation in terms of the fulfillment of the prophecy of Joel: "And in the last days it shall be, God declares, that I will pour out my Spirit upon all flesh, and your sons and your daughters shall prophesy, and your young men shall see visions, and your old men shall dream dreams" (Acts 2:17 quoting Joel 2:28).

In fact, running through the New Testament there is a considerable suspicion of signs and wonders in the sense of the miraculous. The lesson seems to be that God is not a magician performing tricks for the amazement of the credulous. There are warnings against the signs and wonders of false prophets: "False Christs and false prophets will arise and show signs and wonders to lead astray, if possible, the elect" (Mark 13:22); "The coming of the lawless one by the activity of Satan will be with all power and with pretended signs and wonders" (2 Thess. 2:9). Jesus himself is represented as showing a certain impatience with those who look for a sign: "Why does this generation seek a sign? Truly, I say to you, no sign shall be given to this generation" (Mark 8:12). In the fourth gospel John quotes Jesus as saying to the official whose son was ill: "Unless you see signs and wonders you will not believe" (John 4:48)—and this comes in the account of what John describes as "the second sign that Jesus did when he had come from Judaea to Galilee" (John 4:54).

In this way the signs and wonders that accompany the preaching of the Gospel do not seem to be unequivocal demonstrations that allow of no other interpretation than that God is at work. No doubt there were those who were puzzled but remained unconvinced by Jesus' miracles of healing. No doubt there were those in Jerusalem at the first Pentecost who still felt the apostles were drunk. The faith that is demanded by the Gospel has to be a free response to God's free gift of salvation; and for man to be free in making this response he has to be free to turn the other way and reject what God is offering him. It is summed up in the way John records Jesus as rebuking Thomas for failing to believe in his resurrection—a very gentle rebuke, but a rebuke nevertheless: "Blessed are those who have not seen and yet believe" (John 20:29).

All this may suggest that direct awareness of God has no place in the Christian life. But this would be to fail to do justice to the richness and complexity of the Gospel. It is rather that the possibility of direct awareness of God has to be seen in the proper perspective. The normal situation is that "now we see in a mirror dimly," and that it will only be after our death and resurrection in Christ that we shall see "face to face" and "understand fully" even as we have been fully understood (1 Cor. 13:12). But at the same time the mystic experience of God as he is, the piercing of the veil that divides us from God this side of the resurrection, goes back to the first preaching of the Gospel and the first beginnings of the Christian community. Alongside the statements that "no one has ever seen God" (John 1:18, 1 John 4:12) we have to place not only the book of Revelation but the mystic experience of the transfiguration, which has a key place in all three synoptic gospels (Matt. 17:1-8, Mark 9:2-8, Luke 9:28-36), and Paul's account of his own mystical experiences when he is finally driven to revealing them in his attempt to persuade the Christians of Corinth of the legitimacy of his authority as an apostle and the authenticity of the Gospel he is preaching: "And I know that this man was caught up into Paradise—whether in the body or out of the body I do not know, God knows—and he heard things that cannot be told, which man may not utter" (2 Cor. 12:3-4).

So far, then, the implication is that on the one hand mysticism—in the sense of the direct apprehension of God, a kind of foretaste or anticipation of the beatific vision—is not the primary purpose, or even a main purpose, of Christianity, but that on the other hand it does have a definite place within the Christian life as a whole. The ultimate aim of Christianity is of course union with God, but the fulfillment of this aim is for the vast majority of us something eschatological, something that must await the complete establishment of the kingdom. It is not normally something we can expect to experience here and now, on this side of the barrier of death. But when, in rare and exceptional cases, a few Christians do experience in this life the union with God that for the rest of us must wait until after the resurrection, this cannot simply be dismissed as something entirely peripheral to the Christian life, whether of the individual or of the community. The difficulty arises when we try to see what its place is in the Christian scheme of things.

Chapter Three

CLEAR AND DISTINCT IDEAS

There is, however, a threefold difficulty that arises from our situation as Christians living in the western technological culture of the latter half of the twentieth century. As Christians we have to express and live out what we believe in terms of the society we are living in. Our job is not simply to reject absolutely and without qualification the world in which we find ourselves but rather to help towards its redemption, to enable everything that is good in it to flourish and to come to its proper development. It involves a very delicate and paradoxical balance of critical involvement, at one and the same time giving full value to God's judgment upon the world and recognizing that however much it may be improved it will still fall short of the kingdom, while simultaneously being fully involved in every effort to make the world a better place to live in. The Christian needs to be in the vanguard of the revolution while at the same time recognizing that the new society which will emerge from the revolution will not be good enough. It is an attitude that makes the Christian an awkward person to live with for reactionary and revolutionary alike.

This society we live in is marked by what has been

termed the process of secularization. Areas of life, like scientific inquiry, which used to fall within the province of religion, have developed their own autonomy. Far from being a cause for lamentation, marking a turning away from religion, the process of secularization can legitimately be seen as a logical working out of the incarnation and of our redemption through Jesus Christ. It is one aspect of man's liberation from everything that constrained him and held him in bondage.

At the same time, secularization can seem to have made it more difficult for the Christian to believe. No longer is belief in God an automatic and unquestioned assumption underpinning the ordinary person's understanding of the world he lives in. No longer are spiritual forces seen at work in the ordinary events of everyday life. As far as belief is concerned, man is today freer than he was. But at the same time he is freer not to believe.

But the achievements of western technological civilization have not been without their cost. They have come about through concentrating on one particular method of coming to grips with reality—what can be termed the scientific attitude. All this can cope with is what can be measured, what is tangible, what is predictable, what is susceptible to experimental proof, what is quantifiable. Other aspects of reality tend to be ignored because they do not fit into this pattern. The insights into the human condition that come from poetry or from religion are in some strange way devalued and regarded as not being really serious because they are not, and cannot be, expressed in the language of science.[1]

This attitude at once makes mysticism somehow marginal and difficult to square with the rest of our apprehension of reality, which we have become used to considering in this one-dimensional way. At the same time, it gives rise to the second aspect of the threefold difficulty with which we are faced. This is the loss of any sense of God's immediate presence. In the world structured by the language of science, God, quite simply, does not exist. God is a hypothesis that provides an obvious victim for Occam's razor. The god of the philosophers and the god of the gaps have become things of the past. If today we believe in God, this is not because the existence of God is a conclusion to which we are inescapably directed by the facts but because the existence of God offers a satisfactory interpretation of the facts. And, while, for us, believing in God offers what we regard as the only fundamentally satisfactory interpretation of the facts, the only way, ultimately, of making sense of the world we live in rather than regarding it as a random and meaningless jumble of accidents, we have to recognize that other options are possible and that someone is not being either a fool or a knave if he refuses to believe in God but is simply expressing honestly and sincerely how he views the world as he thinks it is.

In this way, both philosophically and practically, God has become more abstract, more remote, less immediate. If we see God at work in the world, whether it is the annual miracle of spring or the reconciliation of a couple on the point of divorce and their discovery of a new and profounder level to their relationship, this is a matter of the interpretation we choose to put on the facts before us. For any event of this kind there is available, at least as a theoretical possibility (because of the frequent impossibility in practice of achieving an exhaustive knowledge of all the facts of a particular case), a logically and rationally convincing explanation in which God is totally irrelevant.

In this way it is difficult for twentieth-century Christians to have any sense of the immediate presence of God without indulging in the kind of schizophrenic approach that keeps religion in one compartment firmly insulated from the rest of life. For us today, God is no longer part of the data. True, if we are Christians it is only because we believe in God that ultimately we can make any kind of satisfying sense out of the data. But God is no longer immediately there. He has become abstract, a matter of deduction and interpretation. We think of him as the ground of our being rather than as the person in whom "we live and move and have our being" (Acts 17:28). Nor is this simply a philosophical point. Theologically we concentrate far more on God as he has revealed himself in the man Jesus Christ than on God the Father himself, and our starting-point is apt to be John's statement that "no man has ever seen God" (1 John 4:12, John 1:18) coupled with the answer he records Jesus as giving to Philip: "He who has seen me has seen the Father" (John 14:9).

This in turn leads on to the third aspect of our three-fold difficulty. If God has become more remote and abstract, prayer becomes a problem. Traditionally, prayer has been defined as the raising up of the heart and mind to God, but it is probably truer to say that most people have thought of it as holding a conversation with God, speaking and talking to God and, it is to be hoped, also trying to listen to what he has to say to us. But to hold a conversation with someone who has become more remote, more abstract, obviously raises difficulties.[2]

And there are difficulties, too, over the subject of our prayer. Many of us were brought up to pray for specific ends or aims. There has even been a noxious tradition among Catholic school-children of praying for success in examinations. But this kind of approach presupposes a God who is always ready to intervene, a kind of heavenly fixer always ready to adjust things on behalf of· his clients, and this is hardly the kind of image of God that any of us can live with. On the face of it, prayer does not seem to have any effect except on our own attitudes. There are, of course, cases where other people's attitudes change for the better, where they become responsive to what we would see as the promptings of the Spirit. But can we say that this is due to our prayer? This would seem to be the most presumptuous and un-Christian arrogance. If we assume, as we must as Christians, that God wills the salvation of all men, then his Spirit is always at work trying to arouse men to an awareness of their situation and of the response they need to make to it.

All three aspects of this triple difficulty raise problems for mysticism. It is not that they rule it out of court completely. It is rather that they tend to reduce it to a peripheral and marginal activity, an aberration even, something that is not in the mainstream of human life and thought and endeavor. In some ways there are parallels between attitudes to mysticism even among those committed to and concerned with Christianity and attitudes to psi phenomena such as extrasensory perception within the world of science. The scientists' chief problem with regard to, say, ESP is not that it does not happen: The trouble is that from time to time it does. The problem is that is does not happen according to a regular and predictable pattern. It is a Cheshire cat phenomenon: It has an awkward habit of disappearing just when one is trying to pin it down. So, too, with mysticism. The mystic or would-be mystic just does not know if he or she will ever attain the summit of mystical experience. It may happen; but most probably the more he or she is concerned about it happening the less likely it is to happen.

Nor is the first aspect of this triple difficulty one that can simply be shelved or put aside by the mere fact of agreeing to discuss questions of religion and thus to go beyond the boundaries of the tangible and the empirical. The itch for precision that has marked what may loosely be termed the scientific attitude has affected our religious attitudes too. Western Christianity in particular has shown a strong disinclination to accept that certain aspects of what we believe are and must remain mysteries, essentially impenetrable to our intellects here and now, things that now we see through a glass darkly and shall only see face to face in the eschatological fulfillment of the kingdom. In this way it seems to be an underlying European attitude of mind that precedes the philosophical development that began with Descartes. The latter's aim was in essence to import into philosophy the certitude of mathematics. But his insistence on clear and certain reasoning led through Locke's insistence on clear and distinct ideas to Hume's famous rejection as "nothing but sophistry and illusion" of everything that was not "abstract reasoning concerning quantity or number" or "experimental reasoning concerning matter of fact and existence." And in turn this led on to the principle of verification—the principle that any proposition that is not either an *a priori* statement or an empirically verifiable hypothesis is literally meaningless—and to the concluding proposition of Wittgenstein's *Tractatus Logico-Philosophicus:* "What one cannot speak about one must keep silent about."

Yet, in reaching this uncomfortable conclusion, Wittgenstein gives the impression of regretting his inability to speak about what nevertheless seems important. The solution to the problem of life may lie in this problem's disappearing like the Cheshire cat, and the answer may lie in the fact that there is no question to be put and therefore no answer; but all the same there is something that cannot be expressed, something that becomes evident, something that *is* what *is* mystical.[3] Nevertheless the answer does not simply lie in pointing out that other modes of discourse exist and have their own validity beyond the rigidly scientific. If a philosopher like A. J. Ayer argues: "If a mystic admits that the object of his vision is something which cannot be described, then he must also admit that he is bound to talk nonsense when he describes it," and goes on to state that in describing his vision the mystic is not giving us any information about the external world but merely "indirect information about the condition of his own mind,"[4] then we have to admit in our turn that this approaches uncomfortably close to a description of the problem of mystical utterance. For what the mystic is trying to describe is "what no eye has seen, nor ear heard, nor the heart of man conceived" (1 Cor. 2:9); he is trying to tell of "things that cannot be told, which man may not utter" (2 Cor. 12:4). If the mystic is unable to tell the rest of us about his experiences, if they are something that cannot in any degree be communicated to or shared with the Christian community as a whole, then it is legitimate to ask if they have any value. It is only what can be shared and communicated that we regard as significant, and the whole object of our redemption in Jesus Christ is to break down the barriers to sharing and communication. In this way mysticism could appear totally irrevelant to the life of the Christian community as a whole.

First, though, it is as well to underline that other modes of discourse beyond the scientific have their own validity. There is the mode of poetry. Whereas scientific discourse aims at precision and the avoidance of ambiguity, striving to ensure that each term carries precisely one and only one meaning, the discourse of poetry revels in ambiguity and in drawing out the overtones and resonances of the multiple meanings that words gather to themselves. This does not mean that poetry should be lacking in precision—far from it. But the precision of poetry is a precision of intuition, not of description. It enables us to see things in a new light by bringing together aspects of reality that in the analytic world of scientific discourse are kept apart. And above all, what *cannot* be said of poetry is that it is meaningless or lacking in significance. It is rather that its meaning is not univocal, like the ideal scientific statement, but multifaceted with layers of meaning built up on each other.

Even more striking is the example of music. Here we have a form of utterance that is meaningful and significant and shows internal coherence and logical development. But it is totally impossible to translate what any piece of music is saying into any kind of verbal description. The first seven bars of Wagner's *Tristan und Isolde,* for example, are definitely saying something; but what they are saying can only be expressed in terms of the music that we hear. Admittedly, we can analyze the music and point out that a chromatic progression on the celli becomes surrounded by a strange harmonic configuration on the woodwind that resolves itself, with a mirror-image of the descending phrase on the celli, into the familiar chord of the dominant seventh; but all that is done by this kind of procedure, which anyway is meaningless without the actual music to refer to, is to make explicit the system of relationships between notes which is what music is all about and which for musicians is, initially at least, a matter of intuition and not conscious analysis.

Music could perhaps in this way stand as a type or example of mystical utterance, something that is undoubtedly meaningful and significant while at the same time resisting translation into the verbal language of everyday life. But it is a strange thing that mystics have not apparently been in the habit of using music to describe their experiences—unless one is prepared to posit some kind of mystical experience as the root of any valid musical utterance. Mystics have chosen to use words to describe their experiences, and this brings us back to our problem.

It is basically the problem underlying any religious

discourse. It could be termed the problem of the eschatological dimension, and in that description the solution may lie. The focus of Christianity is the promise of the future, but it is a future that we cannot yet perceive. We believe that we are promised the eternal life of the kingdom, but we cannot in any meaningful way describe the kind of life this eternal life will be. We can only proceed by analogy, while at the same time taking great care not to become imprisoned or pinned down by our analogies. In the same way, when we are talking about God we are talking about someone we do not and cannot comprehend. At the same time, while we have to admit that we are talking about what we do not at the moment understand, we are bound to assert that it is something we shall understand: We shall know even as also we are known.

In this way, our language can be seen as an indication, a pointer, rather than a description. We are saying that the goal towards which we are on pilgrimage is a goal worth reaching, that it will fulfill and indeed exceed and confound our expectations. But what we cannot do is describe the goal. This means, among other things, that we always have to bear in mind the provisional nature of our discourse as Christians. What we are talking about is the not yet, and it is something we cannot pin down. And, for all that the mystic is someone for whom the not yet has momentarily at least become the here and now, this is something that applies with even greater strength to his utterances.

What he has to say is a pointer towards what we should all be aiming at, what we hope awaits us all, not an exact description. This does not mean that it is value-less. It is rather, as Aristotle pointed out a long time ago, that one should only look for that degree of precision that a subject is capable of.

Chapter Four

THE PROBLEM OF PRAYER

If, as I suggested in the last chapter, the fact that God has become more remote from us, more abstract, has helped to make the very idea of prayer more difficult for us, it may simply be that we have been grasping the wrong end of the stick. Our predicament may be similar to that of the Egyptian hermit Sarapion whose story Cassin tells in his *Conferences*. Like many of his fellow monks in the desert, Sarapion interpreted the statement of Genesis that "God created man in his own image" (Gen. 1:27) to imply that God had a human form, and when the bishop of Alexandria denounced this heresy of anthropomorphism he and the others rejected the bishop's letter. Eventually, however, a deacon named Photinus managed to persuade him that this was not the case and that this was not how this text should be interpreted. But, when the whole group of monks were praying together in thanksgiving for the fact that a hermit of such piety and austerity had been restored to orthodoxy, their prayers were interrupted by "the most bitter weeping and frequent sobs" from Serapion, who burst out with the lamentation: "They have taken my God away from me, and I do not possess him whom I now hold, nor do I know any longer whom I should adore or pray to."[1]

The point is that God never was present in the world in the sense of being like someone to whom one could always turn for a helping hand whenever one was stuck. God does not work in that way. Our realization of his presence in the world is the interpretation we as believers choose to put on the facts we observe, facts which others who are not believers will interpret in a different way that does not involve God and for which in any case an explanation that does not involve God is not only possible but in some sense essential. It is only if we see the world in the light of faith that we become aware of the presence of God. But it can be a disturbing process to realize that God is not there in the same kind of way that, if we are married, our husband or wife is there to provide help or stimulation or comfort or love or even irritation. It is what Karl Rahner has called the "realization of troubled atheism" which, at the same time, he describes as "fundamentally only the growth of God in the spirit of mankind," the "realization that God does not belong within the world-view, that the real God is not a Demiurge, that he is not the spring in the clockwork of the world, that wherever anything happens in the world which forms part of the 'normal' make-up of the world it is always possible to discover for it a cause which is not God himself." And Rahner sums up the situation by saying: "We are just discovering today that one cannot picture God to oneself in an image that has been carved out of the wood of the world."[2]

Normally, then, we encounter God at second hand,

as it were. In the life of the Church the sacraments today are commonly presented as encounters with God; but God is encountered through the medium of signs and symbols, and while we believe that Christ is truly present in the Eucharist, we are a long way from the crude ideas of a purely physical presence that underlay such medieval legends as those of bleeding hosts. If what someone else says or does reveals to us the truth of our situation and the demands that are being made upon us in that situation, then here, too, we encounter God; but again it is an encounter at one remove, through what other people are doing. If the joys and splendors of the natural world move us to wonder at the glory and beauty of it all, then that, too, we can see as an encounter with God—the realization that what has been created is not only good but is hinting at greater good to come, that "all shall be well, and all manner of things shall be well."

And the God we encounter in this way is not a God who can be pinned down. He is a God who is leading us on into a future we cannot predict for ourselves. The solution he offers for our difficulties is radically different from anything we could have worked out for ourselves. For the ultimate and inescapable difficulty of death he offers not any direct denial of death, not any prolongation or amelioration of this life, but the transcending of death in the resurrection. Death itself remains. It is a fate we all have to undergo, and it is a fate God himself accepted in the person of Jesus Christ.

But in accepting it, he changed its meaning so that it is no longer an absolute end to life but a point of radical transformation beyond anything we are capable of conceiving.

Yet we continually try to pin God down within the categories that are familiar to us. Luke records the apostles as urging Jesus, even after the resurrection, to restore the Davidic kingdom to Israel (Acts 1:6). We think we know what we want, unaware that what God is leading us towards is infinitely greater.

All this already suggests a clue to overcoming the difficulties we naturally feel about prayer. We are apt to think of prayer in terms of asking. (The root meaning of the Latin word *precor,* from which our word "pray" is derived, is in fact "to ask," while oddly enough the Greek verb *eukhomai* seems to have more to do with boasting.) Yet if we start from our encounter with God, however much at second hand it may be, asking is hardly our immediate reaction. Our response is surely rather one of wonder and gratefulness. This suggests that it may be more helpful if we begin by thinking of prayer in terms of praise and thanksgiving, to use the traditional language. If we recognize that God is somehow at work and present in the world in which we live, however much our recognition of his activity and presence may be a matter of deduction and interpretation of the factual data of that world, then praise and thanksgiving fall into place as an immediate and spontaneous response.

But at the same time, it is a world where praise and thanksgiving can, to put it at its mildest, seem wildly out of place. It is a world where men and women exploit each other and treat each other with unbelievable cruelty. If, despite the problem of evil and suffering, and with full awareness of the evil and suffering that seems almost built into the structure of the world, we can go on believing in God, then our response will be more sober and chastened. It will tend to be a response of anxious self-examination, of trying to find out what part we have played and are playing in creating the suffering we see around us and asking ourselves what we can do towards bringing it to an end. The demands of the Gospel, the obligation to respond to our neighbor in need, are borne in upon us.

In this way, the world represents a call to action. But we know only too well how easy it is to make matters worse both for ourselves and for others: The road to hell is paved with good intentions. We need to make sure that we are not exploiting someone else in the guise of helping them. We need to strip off the layer upon layer of self-deception that can mask our true motives from ourselves. We have to liberate ourselves from the unconscious as well as the conscious greeds and distortions and fears that affect our judgment and our action so that we can become truly free to respond to the demands of the Gospel.

This may sound like a prescription for Freudian psychoanalysis; and in some cases that or its equivalent may be what is needed. But it is a prescription that runs through Christian ascetic literature. It is what is meant by the insistence on "purity of heart" as the means whereby the monk can gain the kingdom of heaven to be found right at the start of Cassian's *Conferences*.[3] It is something Cassian reports the Abbot Moses as equating with Paul's insistence on the primacy of charity and the way in which "love does not insist on its own way, it is not irritable or resentful, it does not rejoice at wrong" (1 Cor. 13:5-6).[4] It means striving to see things as they really are and to respond to the real demands of the situation, not to what we would like the situation to demand of us. It can be thought of as trying to see things as God sees them, not in any spirit of boastfulness or superiority but because to see things as God sees them is to see them as they really are. It means living up to Jesus' injunction: "You must be perfect, as your heavenly Father is perfect" (Matt. 5:48).

We are driven on, then, to acquiring self-knowledge; and it is here, surely, that prayer, in the sense of asking, comes in. However much we may try to remain open to other people's views both of ourselves and of the world as a whole, we still run up against obstacles. There are habits, obsessions, and fears that blind us to reality; there are patterns of response that we cannot break free from. The process of dealing with this kind of difficulty is, of course, all of a part with the whole business of living in the world and relating to and inter-reacting with other people; and, as we have seen, it is in this that we can become aware of God's presence and activity. But over and above this normal support and encouragement and assistance that comes simply from being a human being (and thus someone related to other human beings), and over and above the exceptional assistance some of us may find ourselves driven to obtaining through a course of psychoanalysis or some other kind of psychiatric therapy, there will still be a need for help. We find ourselves asking for grace—a difficult term these days, though it can be easy enough to have a rough idea of what is meant. We are all aware of occasions when we somehow manage to do better than we could have expected—the kind of situation that is indicated when we say of someone that he seems to be inspired. Grace is that kind of assistance, something that helps us do better than we know we could have done unaided. How it operates is a mystery, and attempts to unravel the mystery have littered the Church's history with vicious theological controversies. But it seems to involve a realistic recognition of one's own shortcomings and inabilities together with a willingness to try to do whatever needs to be done. And however mysterious its operation, it is, for the Christian believer, a reality.

In this manner, we can build up a pattern of prayer and a way of understanding what we are doing when we pray that seems to make sense in the context of twentieth-century life. There is praise and thanksgiving. There is examination of conscience and the continual attempt to do better, to become perfect even as our father in heaven is perfect. There is prayer to God to inspire us and others to do what is right—"thy will be done, thy kingdom come." It is in fact all summed up in the Lord's prayer, which, after all, is the normative and fundamental Christian prayer. Indeed, one of the best forms of prayer, advocated throughout the Church's history, is simply to pray the Lord's prayer, not just uttering it mentally or vocally but trying all the time to understand all that is contained in its deceptively simple phrases and to unwrap the profundity of its meaning.

Prayer, too, can be seen as the essential element in the life of any Christian. It is difficult, if not impossible, to be a Christian, as it were, by instinct. It demands reflection on what we are and what we are about. And this reflection needs to be fed from a number of sources. Of these, as already indicated, the Lord's prayer is the most fundamental. But beyond this we need to be continually imbued with what we can learn from the Bible about God's revelation of himself, both in the history of the people of Israel and ultimately and definitively in the man Jesus. The Bible, too, forms a central part of the Church's public worship, and our experience of the liturgy will react on our private prayer, just as our private prayer will affect the kind of contribution we can make to the worship of the community. (There cannot, in fact, be any hard and fast

43

distinction between public and private prayer. The two flow into each other.) And beyond the Bible there is the whole corpus of Christian literature to be explored—an immense field where every Christian can count on finding something that speaks directly to him and to his condition in a way that other writings preferred by other Christians do not. Some people may derive a benefit from, say, Augustine that they cannot from Francis de Sales; for others it may be the opposite way round. It is all a question of personal temperament.

Personal temperament, in fact, needs to be taken into account with regard to prayer to a much greater extent than has thought to have been the case. Prayer is, after all, a personal matter. It is the core of the Christian's efforts to become the kind of person he or she is meant to be, the kind of person God wants him to become. This suggests that what it does not involve is the kind of discipline that simply cuts across the grain and tries to force someone into a pattern that is uncongenial to him. In the recent past, there was too much of this in the Catholic Church. Those who found, say, the recitation of the rosary uncongenial were regarded as to a considerable extent un-Catholic, disloyal. There was little attempt to suggest that they might enjoy trying to pray the psalms. The same kind of thing applied to the liturgy: If a pontifical high Mass with all the trimmings left one unmoved and what one was really hankering after was the kind of face-to-face, small group, low Church liturgy that has now become possible as a result of Vatican II, then again one wasn't really a true dyed-in-the-wool Catholic. And the same applies in reverse: It is in the highest degree unChristian to sneer at people because they find that the rosary is for them a genuine means of prayer or because they find a sung Latin Mass in the Tridentine rite a truer stimulus to devotion than any available English liturgy.

Chapter Five

THE CLOUD OF UNKNOWING

So we can see how prayer is an indispensable element in the life of any Christian without feeling that we are giving up the struggle to express what we believe in terms that are valid today or simply dropping back into medieval categories. Our response to the Gospel has to be a conscious response, and prayer is the expression of this conscious awareness of what the Gospel demands of us. It is a process of reflection on what the Gospel means and an affirmation that what the Gospel promises and offers us transcends the necessarily limited boundaries within which we live. Despite everything, there is a God, and "all shall be well, and all manner of things shall be well." We may not yet be able to perceive the structure and meaning of the apparently random, meaningless, and often cruel jumble of events of which we form a part. But we are able to grasp the assurance that there is a structure and meaning to be unfolded.

In itself, however, prayer is a long way from mysticism. Prayer is still very much something that we do, whereas the mystical experience is something that God does; it is, as it were, a taking over of the mystic by God without the mystic's personality being destroyed in the process. If we think of prayer as talking to God, mysticism is very much a matter of listening. But prayer is the indispensable foundation for any mystic. Indeed, what the mystic experiences can be thought of as a form of prayer, but one that is no longer a matter of conscious effort and struggle. The founding father of monasticism, Antony of Egypt, is reported to have said that prayer can only be described as perfect when the person praying is no longer conscious of himself or of his prayer.[1] And Abbot Isaac, in what forms one of the earliest treatises on prayer and the mystical life, is recorded by Cassian as insisting on the Pauline injunction to "pray constantly" (1 Thess. 5:17) and as defining the goal of perfection, what we are to aim at if we are to be "perfect, as our heavenly Father is perfect" (Matt: 5:48), as "the daily raising and abstracting of the mind from all earthly longings to spiritual things, to such an extent that all its life and concern, all the heart's activity become one single and continuous prayer".[2] The state of pure prayer he later describes as one "which is not only not taken up by the consideration of any visual image but is not marked by any oral or verbal activity; rather, the mind's attention has caught fire, through an indescribable ecstasy of the heart, and the prayer is carried forward by an insatiable keenness of the spirit and becomes something which the mind, borne beyond all sensation and all visible things, pours forth to God with sighs and groans too deep for words."[3]

47

Understandably, mystical writers do not really have very much to tell us about the highest states of mystical prayer. What they are talking about is something that transcends ordinary human experience—something therefore for which ordinary human language is more than ordinarily inadequate. What is involved is some kind of union between the human soul or personality and God. It is not something that is in any way dependent upon the person who devotes himself to prayer and the efforts he may make to reach this state: "It is never attained by study, but only by grace," says the anonymous fourteenth-century author of *The Cloud of Unknowing*.[4] Teresa of Avila makes the same kind of point with her famous simile of the four ways of watering a garden in the somewhat arid conditions of Spain: First the "very laborious" method of drawing water up from a well, then the less laborious method of using a water-wheel and buckets to draw water, then irrigation from a stream or a spring, and finally "by heavy rain, when the Lord waters it himself without any labour of ours".[5] There is a steady progression from what one can do oneself to what can only be done by God.

But, if the attainment of the heights of mystical prayer is something essentially outside the mystic's control, that does not mean just sitting back and waiting for something to happen that may or may not take place. Mystical experience may be the product of grace, but it seems something that will only occur if it is prepared for and striven towards. Grace and human effort do not cancel each other out but are complementary. The anonymous author of the *Cloud* counselled his reader to strike "that thick cloud of unknowing" that veils the essential incomprehensibility of God from the human soul "with the sharp dart of longing love."[6] Just as in Paul's famous hymn of love, in which he tries to show the Corinthians "a still more excellent way", it is a situation where the mind has to cease from its restless probings and give way to love alone, since love alone can be perfect: "Love never ends; as for prophecies, they will pass away; as for tongues, they will cease; as for knowledge, it will pass away. For our knowledge is imperfect and our prophecy is imperfect; but when the perfect comes, the imperfect will pass away" (1 Cor. 13:8-10). The effort and striving have to be to *cease* from all effort and striving, at last to keep still and actually to listen to what God has to say instead of filling one's awareness with what in this context can only be idle chatter.

This in turn demands a constant effort to purify oneself. It is something, for example, on which Abbot Isaac is reported by Cassian as insisting continually, and, from that day to this, most worthwhile writing on prayer has been full of advice on how to achieve this purification. It involves the mystic in freeing himself or herself from all attachment to and entanglement in the things of this world. Obviously no human being can become a disembodied spirit, and in fact Christians do

not and cannot look forward to a non-physical existence, to being freed from the body; they look forward
to the resurrection of the body, to its being transformed
and transcended in the eternal life of the kingdom. But
the mystic has to learn to detach himself not only from
purely physical desires and longings but from all the
subtler attachments that can crowd in upon him, from
concerns and anxieties which may be good and praise-
worthy in themselves but which can only create a further barrier between him and God. It is a stripping
away of all the accretions which have gathered to defend and occupy the person so as to leave the essential
core of personality naked before its creator. It is, understandably, by all accounts a long, tortuous and painful
process, analyzed by John of the Cross as the dark
night of the senses and the dark night of the spirit.[7]

It is a road full of pitfalls, obstacles, and wrong turn-
ings that can mislead the unwary. That is why so much
of mystical literature is taken up with explaining what
is involved in this process and how the would-be mystic
can discern whether or not he or she is on the right
road. It is only too easy for the person concerned to become side-tracked and remain content with a kind of
spiritual narcissism—with contemplating his own image, the ideas and emotions thrown up by his subcon-
scious, and falling in love with it. Unless he can break
free from this temptation and recognize illusions of
this kind for what they are he will never rise any
higher and may even succeed in damaging or destroy-

ing himself through a kind of spiritual self-indulgence. This explains why John of the Cross comes down so strongly against visions and similar sense-impressions, and even against private revelations of a more spiritual nature.[8] They are at best stages on the road, and someone who confuses each successive milepost with his destination will never reach the end of his journey.

It is also an intensely personal journey. Teresa of Avila may give the impression in her autobiography that the eighteen years she spent as a nun before she was able genuinely to pray could have been substantially cut short if she had had the benefit of a wise and learned spiritual director. But one cannot help wondering to what extent this would have been true. In prayer, as in every other department of life, we learn by our mistakes, and there is a limit to the extent to which we can be helped by others. Particularly is this so when what is involved is the process of learning to be oneself. This may sound paradoxical, since the practice of mystical prayer demands the stripping away of every trace of self-regard and self-consideration. But the aim of this stripping away is to leave the essential core of personality free genuinely to know and to love God. What it got rid of is everything that stands in the way of responding immediately and spontaneously to the love of God. The path of mystical prayer is thus a search for God that is also a search for oneself. It is the living out of Augustine's dictum that God has "made us for yourself, and our heart is troubled until it rests in you."[9] Only in finding God can we find ourselves.

There are thus differences of approach. What suits one person may not suit another. "As there are many mansions in heaven, so there are many roads leading to them," says Teresa of Avila when she corrects herself after describing meditation on Christ's sufferings as "a most excellent and safe path for all" and goes on to mention other suitable subjects for meditation.[10] There is indeed a contrast between the value that Teresa places on visions and locutions and the cautious indifference recommended by John of the Cross. (Any contradiction between the two is more apparent than real, since John's aim is to explain how one may reach union with God, and Teresa points out that visions and locutions are never, in her view, experienced when the soul is in union.)[11] There is a contrast between the insistence on the essential incomprehensibility of God we find running through *The Cloud of Unknowing* and Julian of Norwich's enjoyment of being looked after by "our tender Mother Jesus".[12]

It is even possible to speculate that what each mystic experiences depends on his or her individual personality. This is hardly surprising. There is a sense in which each of us in this life experiences our own individual world, different from anyone else's. The basic external data are of course the same for all of us, but there are subtle variations—and sometimes important differences—in how we see and interpret them. What we experience is thus to a very small but yet significant extent an expression of our own personality, a projection outwards of our own individual frame of reference. And it seems reasonable to suppose that we shall all experience heaven in the same way. It will be the same heaven, but each will experience it according to his or her own personality. At the same time it seems equally reasonable to suppose that the barriers to communication will at last be down and that we shall be able fully to share our individual and unique experiences. Added to this, our idea of heaven implies the fulfillment and completion of each individual personality, no longer stunted and distorted by the evil that forms an inescapable part of human existence.

If we regard what the mystics experience as a foretaste of heaven, of the beatific vision, then it is only natural that what different mystics experience show differences of emphasis. The only thing is that what they experience remains essentially incommunicable, beyond saying that it is a direct experience of God and of the love of God.

Finally, the mystic's road can be seen as an obsessive search for truth. What the mystic needs above everything else is to "know even as also he is known" (1 Cor. 13:12)—to know God and to know himself. It is a search for truth as obsessive as that of Oedipus, who penetrated the tissue of evasions and prevarications spun by those around him to arrive at the final shattering revelation of the truth about himself. This obsessive longing for God as he is would seem an essential part of the make-up of any mystic. Without it, his prayer would remain on the level of meditation on what God has done for us and reflection on what God demands of us. Most of us have moments of wanting to get to the bottom of things, of making a serious effort to face up to ourselves as we really are. But there are very, very few of us who are prepared to make this kind of activity the center of our lives, who are obsessed with the need to penetrate to the heart of the mystery of the human condition. Those who are, are the mystics.

Chapter Six

ELITIST ESCAPISM?

Despite all this, many Christians today may still not feel entirely happy about mysticism. They may quite well accept occasional involuntary mystical experiences, which in fact would seem to be commoner than might be suspected: A survey carried out in the spring of 1972, according to a recent report quoting the sociologist Andrew Greeley, revealed that "36 per cent of the American population say that they have at some time in their lives felt as though they were very close to a powerful force that seemed to lift them out of themselves."[1] It could well be, in fact, that mysticism not only resembles extrasensory perception in being a Cheshire cat phenomenon that cannot be pinned down, is unpredictable in its occurrence beyond some very broad statistical probability, and cannot be regularly made to happen in anything approaching laboratory conditions but, that like ESP phenomena, the potential ability for it may be more widely spread than can be realized in a culture that does not place great value on such things.

However, the obsessional pursuit of union with God which is what the mystic devotes himself to can seem a rather dubious occupation. It can be regarded as turning one's back on the world instead of working out one's salvation in and through this world—as seems to be demanded by the essentially incarnational quality of Christianity. (And because mysticism demands an overriding obsession with penetrating to the ultimate truth whatever the cost, it is necessarily an occupation confined to a relatively select few.) Of mysticism, above all, it is true that "many are called, but few are chosen" (Matt. 22:14). This contrasts sharply with our present awareness that God "desires all men to be saved and to come to the knowledge of the truth" (1 Tim. 2:4) and our rediscovery of the way in which salvation involves us not just as separate individuals but as a community, as the people of God. In fact, by one of those paradoxes of the Church's intellectual history, these days we place greater stress on God's gift of salvation to his people as a whole and on the way in which we as individuals are saved as members of a community than in the days of ecclesiastical triumphalism and institutional boasting when a more individualistic approach to salvation was the rule. Leading on from this consideration is the disquiet that can be caused if the mystic is seen as somehow opting out of the community structure and developing his own private covenant of salvation with God by establishing a direct and unmediated relationship with him.

To take these objections in order, there is first the business of turning one's back on the world. The trouble here, is that built into the Christian tradition we have inherited there is an insistence on contempt for the world that today jars on our sensibilities. True, it was often carried to absurd lengths, and the impression given by some medieval writers is that they had a hard job of it to persuade themselves, let alone anyone else, that the world really was the horrible place they made it out to be.[2] But, even bearing in mind the extraordinary ambivalance and ambiguity with which the term "world" is used in the New Testament, it is an attitude that finds some striking backing in the Gospels. Jesus is reported by Luke as using some very strong language indeed: "If anyone comes to me and does not hate his own father and mother and wife and children and brothers and sisters, yes, and even his own life, he cannot be my disciple" (Luke 14:26). This is not the world in the sense of the miasma of wrong-doing and evil in which we are inevitably and inextricably involved through the mere fact of being human and from which Jesus has come to liberate us (the sense, for example, that we find so frequently in John's Gospel) but the world in the sense of the primary human relationships of love and support. Jesus was addressing an audience for whom God himself had spoken from Sinai to command them to "honor your father and your mother, that your days may be long in the land which the Lord your God gives you" (Exodus 10:12)—a commandment that stands first of those dealing with behavior towards other people. No doubt he had to exaggerate in order to drive the point home to such an audience, and we may well prefer Matthew's gentler formulation: "He who loves father or mother more than me is not worthy of me; and he who loves son or daughter more than me is not worthy of me" (Matt. 10:37). But we are still left with the uncomfortably scandalous and subversive teaching Jesus was proclaiming in these passages. We are called on to break free from the whole network of human society and from the conventions and values it imposes on us. The point is clearer if we remember the all-embracing quality of the kind of value-system encouraged by the extended family of Jesus' day, when belonging to and being supported by a wide family network was to a considerable extent essential for survival. But we must not go along with this system. We must turn our backs on it and place the Gospel first (Ps. 137:5-6):

> If I forget you, O Jerusalem,
>   let my right hand wither!
> Let my tongue cleave to the roof of my mouth,
>   if I do not remember you,
> if I do not set Jerusalem
>   above my highest joy!

The fundamental point is that it is the Gospel which must judge the world, not the world the Gospel. Nothing must be allowed to come between us and God. Anything in this life can all too easily distract us from God, can encourage us to turn aside from the painful attempt to live out the demands of love in all their fullness. It is a question of priorities, of seeing things in the right perspective. True, there is also the fundamental fact that this world is good in itself, that it is not only created and upheld but redeemed by God. And it can lead us to God. But it can also lead us away from God. It is ambivalent, and to be able to cope with it without running the risk of being destroyed by it we have to see it in the right perspective by putting God first.

Put this way, the tradition of contempt of the world may still cut across our aching need for the familiar comfort of things known and loved, but it becomes easier for us to grasp today than the harsh and forbidding language of the Roman missal when, in the post-communion for the second Sunday in Advent, we ask God to teach us "to despise the things of earth and love the things of heaven." How many of us today can sincerely make this prayer? Again, how many of us can take a spiritual writer like Francis de Sales seriously when he tells us to resolve to "despise the world?"[3] It is the language of Luke rather than that of Matthew; and it is the latter we are happier with these days, since there we can find a recognition that human loves have their place provided they do not challenge our love of God. After all, it is only through the things of this world, through our experience of love and reconciliation in our relationships with other people, that so many of us are drawn, however hesitatingly, towards God.

Yet even the good things of this life must be thrust from him by the mystic. Indeed, in the writings of the mystics one finds a clearer recognition than in much spiritual writing of the goodness of what one must thrust away from oneself if one seeks to know and love God alone. That, no doubt, is because they are writing for people who are already able to cope with the more ordinary temptations of greed or anger or envy or lust and who must now learn to put a "cloud of forgetting" between themselves "and the whole created world."[4]

But this does not mean that the good things of this world are absolutely to be despised in themselves. What is involved is a greater awareness that they are not ends in themselves, that everything is relative except God who is the measure everything is related to. Once they are seen in this perspective, then they can be used and enjoyed. It is the Christian tradition of detachment, of recalling that "here we have no lasting city" (Heb. 13:14) and that the things we use and enjoy here and now are the means we use to make this stage or that of our pilgrimage towards "the city which is to come." Without them we should never set out, never reach the end even of an early stage of our journey; but we must not confuse them with, or let them distract us from, the ultimate goal we are somehow making our way towards. To do so would be like someone climbing a mountain confusing a hump on an outlying ridge with the summit itself.

In this way what the mystic is learning to do is how

to live in this world and play a full part in it without running the risk that most of us run of being distracted and led astray. In fact, what is noteworthy about so many mystics—and this answers the second objection —is the remarkably active life they manage to lead. Teresa of Avila could hardly have launched the Carmelite reform simply by locking herself in her cell and by doing that *first* that she was able to undertake the contemplating God as he is in himself. But it was only work that is her practical memorial. Even an anchoress like Julian of Norwich gives the impression of having always been ready to share her wisdom with others, to the extent of entertaining pious gossips like Margery Kempe. In our own day someone like Thomas Merton has been able to combine the practice of contemplation with active concern over the horrifying injustices of the post-war world; and undoubtedly, of the many prophetic voices to be heard in the Church of recent years, his was among the most effective.

What seems to happen with the mystic is that through discovering God and thereby, as we have seen, discovering himself, he is released from all (or at least the vast majority of) the tensions and anxieties and inhibitions that continually prevent the rest of us from exerting our full potential. Nor is his knowledge of God some esoteric secret to be hugged to himself. Rather is it the underpinning of his whole life and work. True, it is hardly something he can share directly with others. But he is aware that the fleeting knowledge of God he has been granted is a foretaste of what awaits all men in the kingdom and so what he has been granted he can to some extent share by helping and encouraging others to strive in their own way towards the kingdom while—as the many writings of mystics bear witness—he is always ready to put his own experience at the service of those others who have the gift and the will to follow the same path as himself.

Thus the mystic does not cut himself off from the community. True, the practice of mystical prayer is something essentially solitary and individual. It is anything but a shared experience, and for it the mystic has to withdraw from the world—as indeed Jesus told us all to do when we pray: "Go into your room and shut the door and pray to your Father who is in secret" (Matt: 6:6). But the withdrawal is followed by a return. Indeed, for the historian Arnold Toynbee mysticism is the chief example of the process of withdrawal and return. It is:

A disengagement and temporary withdrawal of the creative personality from his social milieu, and his subsequent return to the same milieu transfigured: In a new capacity and with new powers. The disengagement and withdrawal make it possible for the personality to realize individual potentialities which might have remained in abeyance if the individual in whom they were immanent had not been released for a moment from his toils and trammels. The withdrawal is an opportunity, and perhaps a necessary condition, for the anchorite's transfiguration; but, by the same token, this transfiguration can have no purpose, and perhaps even no meaning, except as a prelude to the return of the transfigured personality into the social milieu out of which he has originally come: A native environment from which the human social animal cannot permanently estrange himself without repudiating his humanity and becoming 'either a beast or a god' (Aristotle, *Politics*, 1253A). The return is the essence of the whole movement, as well as its final cause.[5]

This is mysticism as known by its fruits. As Christians we may put it a different way round, but the effect is the same. We may say that the mystic strives single-mindedly to know and love God as he is, and that the knowledge and love of God impel him back to love and serve God in his creation.

But, if the mystic does not cut himself off from the community, he and his fellows can still be regarded as forming a spiritual élite, a sort of Church within the Church, as if they are the only ones who really know what it is all about and the rest of us are mere camp-followers or outsiders. This kind of attitude can easily be fostered by the way in which the religious life was traditionally labelled the "state of perfection", with the clear implication that there were those who really took the Gospel seriously and strove to become perfect even as our heavenly Father is perfect and those who did not, making a distinction, as it were, between first and second-class Christians.[6] It was an attitude fostered too by consideration of the story of Mary and Martha with Jesus' remark that "only one thing is needed" and his assurance that "Mary has chosen the good portion, which shall not be taken away from her"

(Luke 10:38-42). In the past, readers of this passage seem to have identified, or wanted to identify, with Mary. Today we find ourselves automatically identifying and sympathizing with Martha—especially if we have ever found ourselves slaving away in the kitchen while other members of the family have been sitting around reading or watching television or listening to records or the radio oblivious of all the chores demanding to be done. For us the "one thing needful" and "the good portion" that Mary has chosen have become among the hard sayings of the Gospel we find it difficult to come to terms with.

Now what is interesting about this story is that Luke tells it as a pendant to the story of the good Samaritan. In its context it comes after that strongest possible reminder of the overriding duty of responding automatically and without thinking of ourselves to the needs of our fellowmen. And that in its turn is an amplification of Jesus's evasive answer to the lawyer's question: "What shall I do to inherit eternal life?" when, as we have seen, Jesus balances love of God and love of neighbor and insists that we must fulfill both loves. What Christianity so often presents us with is a "both/and" where, because we are limited in time and space and can only do or think of one thing at a time, we look for an "either/or." We expect simple answers to complex problems, and when we are faced with a "both/and" we are always tempted to interpret it as an "either/or."

64

This, in fact, seems to be what is liable to happen in our reading of this story. We want to simplify it to mean that contemplation is all that matters, and to hell with doing the washing-up. But what Jesus seems to be saying is to warn us both not to pass by on the other side and, if we are able to act the good Samaritan, not to expect everyone else to pitch in and help. Other people have their part to play in their own way, and we must not expect them to follow our particular idea of what needs to be done. We must get on with our own job and let others get on with theirs without expecting them to do ours for us. In this way the story of Martha and Mary is a reminder that we must leave other people free to work out their own salvation in their own way. We are all different, and we must allow other people to be different without envying them their gifts or feeling that they ought to be doing things in our way. In other words, what we all need is humility, and the ability to love other people as they are and not as we think they ought to be.

It is a lesson driven home by Paul with his reminders that "there are varieties of gifts, but the same Spirit", that we are all members of one body and that it would be ridiculous if we all wanted to make a different contribution to the life of the Church from the one we are able and called on to make (1 Cor. 12:4-31)—a passage, incidentally, that leads on to the "still more excellent way" he shows in his hymn of love. The answer is that mystics have their place in the Church and are indispensable to its life, but so too do all other Christians with all their very different gifts and abilities and contributions.

Chapter Seven

"A VERY HORRID THING"

There is yet another objection to mysticism which, no doubt, will seem to many contemporary Catholics a positive argument in its favor. This is the suspicion and, on occasions, the hostility with which it has often been regarded by the institutional Church. Many mystics have, of course, been recognized as saints, while others—notably John of the Cross, Teresa of Avila, and Catherine of Siena—have indeed been proclaimed doctors of the Church. Yet even someone of the stature of John of the Cross could arouse doubts in official minds. Despite careful editing of the first incomplete publication of his works, forty propositions were extracted from this 1618 edition and presented to the Spanish Inquisition for condemnation on the grounds that his teaching was identical with that of the Illuminists of Alumbrados, a mystical sect with heretical leanings which the Inquisition was at pains to suppress during the sixteenth and seventeenth centuries. "The attempt would probably have succeeded," notes the mystic's translator, E. Allison Peers, "but for the warm, vigorous and learned defense put up by the Augustinian Fray Basilio Ponce de León, a theological professor in the University of Salamanca."[1] Even after

John of the Cross had been beatified (1675) and canonized (1726) an attempt to publish a complete and unexpurgated edition of his works fell through in the latter half of the eighteenth century—among other things, because the Carmelite censors felt the order's credit would suffer if it became known that earlier Carmelite editors had suppressed passages of his works. It was only in the twentieth century that a full scholarly edition of this mystic's writings became available.

The posthumous suspicion John of the Cross had to endure (he died in 1591) was paralleled earlier by mystics of the German Dominican school in the fourteenth century. In 1329, twenty-eight propositions culled from the writings and sermons of Meister Eckhart were condemned, seventeen of them as heretical, the other eleven as giving a bad impression, temerarious, and suspect of heresy (DS 950-980). But the condemnation made the interesting admission that this last group of eleven could provide or contain an orthodox meaning if there were sufficient additional explanation. In 1330, Meister Eckhart's pupil Heinrich Suso had to defend himself against accusations of heresy. Three centuries later, having read such mystics as Jan van Ruysbroeck, Johannes Tauler, and Hendrik Herp seems to have been the major crime that caused Richelieu to imprison Pierre Guérin and the Bucquet brothers in the 1630s.

The kind of remark that upset official minds was

Eckhart's statement that God's glory was made manifest and shone forth in everything that was done, even if it was evil, or his saying: "If someone were to commit a thousand mortal sins, and if this person were of the right disposition, he ought not to wish not to have committed them" (DS 954, 965). The first underlines the way in which mystics concentrate so much on the goodness and love of God that awareness of evil risks becomes blotted out. Julian of Norwich, indeed, was clearly worried about the problem of reconciling the existence of hell with the love and mercy of God. While she asserted her adherence to what "Holy Church teaches me to believe," at the same time she thought it "quite impossible" to reconcile the existence of the damned with God's promise "that everything should turn out well."[2] The second of Eckhart's statements can also be paralleled from Julian: "Moreover God showed that sin need be no shame to a man but can even be worthwhile. For just as every sin has its corresponding penalty because God is true, so the same soul can know every sin to have its corresponding blessing because God is love. Just as various sins are punished with various penalties according to their seriousness, so may they be rewarded with various joys in heaven if they have brought punishment and sorrow to the soul on earth."[3] This may be a little different from Eckhart's point, which is surely the obligation on all of us to accept responsibility for our past and to recognize that often we are led to God precisely by realizing where and how we have gone wrong. But both Eckhart and Julian are emphasizing the Christian paradox that we are called upon to do the impossible.

The difficulties that can arise between mystics and the official Church seem to spring from two main causes. One is the fact that mystics are operating on, or even a little beyond, the frontiers of human speech and understanding. Their language has to be more than usually metaphorical and analogical; and all metaphors and analogies are open to misunderstanding if pushed too far. The other lies in the western Christian tradition of hankering after ever greater precision, of trying always to pin God down more and more exactly. The western European mind seems singularly unable to live with uncertainty, even (or perhaps especially) when uncertainty is all that is possible. This in part explains the disease of creeping infallibility that has affected the Catholic Church. There is, and since the Middle Ages has been, a longing to define what perhaps ought to be left vague and undefined. The resulting overanxiety whether this or that statement is completely orthodox or not can claim mystics as well as theologians among its victims. As we have seen, John of the Cross managed to escape, but apparently only just; while the suspicion would seem to be justified that a thorough study of Eckhart's writings could clear him of the condemnation of 1329.

But there has been more than simply a neurotic anxiety over orthodoxy to the suspicion that mysticism has on occasion aroused on the part of the official institutional Church. One clue lies in the attempt to link John of the Cross with the heretical sect of the Alumbrados. Mysticism can be seen as particularly liable to overbalance into heresy. Any aspect of Christianity can, of course, overbalance into heresy if it is taken out of context and pushed too far. That in fact is what heresy consists of: Not so much a flat denial of this aspect or that of the total complexity of the truth which has been revealed to us in Christ Jesus, but an overemphasis on one aspect to such an extent as to introduce a distortion. Orthodoxy lies in maintaining the balance, in resisting the temptation to sharpen the "both/and" of Christianity into an "either/or." And there are minor distortions to be found in the writings of any theologian universally recognized as orthodox; what Augustine had to say about original sin, for example, needs to be balanced by what his eastern contemporaries, unaffected by the demands of the Pelagian controversy, were saying on the subject, while both sets of fourth-century views need to be read and understood within the context of their times. For this reason, any interpretation of the Gospel has to be placed within the context of the views of the entire Christian community in its extension both through space and through time—with the further proviso that even our total understanding of the Gospel, although adequate for our needs at the moment, still falls short of the complete understanding we shall be granted in the king-

dom and is always capable of further refinement as
God leads his people on their as yet unfinished pilgrimage.

Mysticism, from this point of view, offers particularly strong temptations. Because it involves an intensely personal and individual struggle there is the
temptation to weaken the bonds with other people.
Because the contemplative life has been traditionally
regarded as in some way higher and superior to other
forms of Christian life there is the temptation to look
down on those who do not possess the gifts without
which the mystical endeavor is doomed to failure.
Because mysticism cuts through the Gordian knot of
agonizing over how we should interpret and respond
to what the Gospel demands of us to arrive at a direct
love and knowledge of God as he is in himself, not
mediated through the necessarily distorting medium of
human words and actions, there is the temptation to
break loose from this essentially incarnational nature
of Christianity, from the fact that the normal way of
salvation is through the contradictory complexities of
human love and suffering. To use a crude and imperfect analogy, mysticism can be thought of as using a
helicopter to reach a mountain top; and the danger
lies in assuming that everyone can use a helicopter and
that those who can't don't deserve to reach the summit, when in fact there are nowhere near enough heli-
copters to go round and most people have to climb
anxiously inch by inch up the rock-face, from hold to
precarious hold.

There is, thus, in mysticism, if taken the wrong way, a danger of élitism, of ignoring that salvation is freely offered to all men without exception and that this offer of salvation takes into account more fully than any of us are able to do the limitations of each person's individual situation. There is also a risk of gnosticism, of making salvation dependent upon some special secret knowledge imparted only to a chosen few. And there is the danger of what can be termed pseudo-mysticism, a gushing enthusiasm that is more a matter of spiritual self-indulgence than the painful and rigorous agony of gradually coming closer and closer to the ultimate truth as, for example, mapped out for us by John of the Cross.

All this can go some way towards explaining the suspicion which mystics have often encountered. The rest of us need to create the kind of climate in which genuine mystics can flourish and make their indispensable contribution to our lives as Christians while at the same time being on our guard against pseudo-mystics and doing our best gently to deflate their pretensions and to prevent them taking themselves too seriously. A certain wariness and scepticism is in order—which means that most difficult of all endeavors, trying to keep a genuinely open mind instead of prejudging the issue one way or another. Above all this is necessary when it comes to claims of any kind of private revelation. "Sir, the pretending to extraordinary revelations and gifts of the Holy Ghost is a horrid thing, a very horrid thing," was how Bishop Butler rebuked John Wesley in the robust language of eighteenth-century England. Although the Anglican bishop was most probably using "pretend" in its now obsolete sense of "claim", we might not put things quite so strongly in these days of the Pentecostalist movement. Yet we still need to be very much on our guard against attempts to elevate any one gift into the one thing necessary or to promote any one form of prayer and devotion into infallible means of salvation.

But over and above this legitimate suspicion and scepticism there can lurk a totally unworthy suspicion of mysticism that at times swings over into positive hostility. This has its roots in the way in which the mystic cuts through all the framework and scaffolding of human interpretations and human institutions to arrive at a direct apprehension of God as he is in himself. For someone who has placed his whole security in the institutional framework, this is a threat. Someone who exaggerates the importance of the Church as the indispensable means of salvation can easily react with something approaching panic if someone else calmly bypasses the whole network of institutions and sacraments and officially approved devotions and suggests by his example that they might not be quite as essential as the first kind of person would like them to be. Such a reminder of the provisional nature of the Church is, to say the least, unwelcome. And the mystic is free. He has something by which he can evaluate the Church and in the light of which he can interpret and understand the message it is the Church's duty to proclaim. For those who attempt to translate the glorious freedom of the sons of God into a new and terrible bondage to law, that is a threat indeed.

This in part explains the swing away from mysticism within the Catholic Church from the eighteenth century onwards and the concentration on forms of devotion that made it difficult to rise above the first, elementary stages of prayer. Devotions do, of course, have their place. Many people, for example, have been helped by thinking of God's limitless love for all men in terms of the sacred heart of Jesus. But to remain at this level, or to remain at the level of meditating on different aspects of Jesus's life and sayings and suffering as recounted in the Gospel, precludes rising to any higher level of prayer. As the author of *The Cloud of Unknowing* puts it: "Indeed, if we may say so reverently, when we are engaged on this work it profits us little or nothing to think even of Gods kindness or worth, or of our Lady, or of the saints or angels, or of the joys of heaven, if you think thereby by such meditation to strengthen your purpose. In this particular matter it will not help at all. For though it is good to think about the kindness of God, and to love him and praise him for it, it is far better to think about him as he is, and to love him and praise him for himself."[4]

There were, of course, other factors at work besides the triumphalism that concentrated on the necessity of defending the Church as institution against the corrosive effects of the Reformation, when a perfectly legitimate insistence on the primacy of scripture and on the rights of the individual conscience could all too easily be taken as threatening the Church's continuity, authenticity, and universality. There was the Quietist controversy. Quietism seems to have involved an over-emphasis on passivity and self-abnegation; and from this it was a short step to the conclusion that the mystic or would-be mystic was somehow beyond good and evil, was no longer bound by the ordinary rules and customs of human behavior. At times there seems to have been the emergence of an almost schizophrenic attitude which dissociated what the mystic did or thought (which could include a great deal reckoned as sin) from his concentration on God. Thus among the sixty-eight propositions which in 1687 led to the condemnation of Miguelde Molinos are two which put forward the intriguing theory that contemplatives who have reached a state of perfection can nevertheless, without any sin or guilt on their part, be moved by the devil to masturbate or fornicate while wide awake and in full possession of their faculties (DS 2241-2). All this was seen as leading to greater contempt of oneself and resignation before God (DS 2243).

Clearly, all this was far from genuine mysticism, even though today we would regard the underlying condition revealed as one needing psychiatric treatment rather than the prisons of the Inquisition. In passing, it is worth noting that in this fashion the case of

Molinos brings out the great underlying danger of attempting to become a mystic: That the process of discovering oneself and trying to get rid of all the neurotic failings standing between oneself and the ability to concentrate on loving and knowing God as he is can bring to light symptoms one is incapable of coping with. The seventeenth century remedy was a good spiritual director, the twentieth century remedy is quite probably a good psychiatrist, whether as well as or instead of a good spiritual director; but in either set of conditions such people, with the wisdom and insight to help others without imposing an alien pattern on them, are rare and difficult to find.

If Quietism had merely represented a desperate attempt by celibates who had been unable to come to terms with the fact of their own sexuality to cope with the persistence of sexual drives that were all the stronger for being suppressed, then it might not have mattered very much. There was more to it than that, as came out in the condemnation of Fénelon in 1699. What quietism did was to exaggerate certain tendencies in orthodox mysticism—the recognition that beyond a certain stage it is less and less a question of the mystic himself doing anything and more and more a question of God taking him over; the need for passivity and resignation when this kind of stage is reached; the need to stop thinking about oneself and what one wanted and was doing. The quietest emphasis on pure disinterested love left any fear of damnation or hope of

eternal reward far behind—to the point where someone could be convinced that he himself was justly
damned. Coupled with this was a disparagement of
all lesser stages of the spiritual life and of the means
of devotion and the often mixed motives with which
ordinary Christians kept themselves going. There was
more than a suggestion that the only Christians worthy
of the name were those capable of practicing the
prayer of quiet. And the insistence on self-abnegation
and on nothingness can, to a modern reader, smack
more of Buddhism than of Christianity (though the
extent of the common ground between Christian and
eastern forms of mysticism is, of course, another and
more difficult question).

Unfortunately, the condemnation of quietism meant
in effect that mysticism itself came under suspicion.
There may well have been other factors at work. Certainly the seventeenth century climate seems to have
encouraged a concentration on the workings on the
internal life which could spill over into the kind of
narcissistic self-absorption we find in Madame Guyon,
that hysterical and enthusiastic woman who was the
catalyst for the great quarrel between Bossuet and
Fénelon and ultimately Fénelon's condemnation at
Rome, and all this was in contrast to the cool rationality
of the following century. But at all events, mysticism
entered on a virtual decline within the Catholic
Church, only to emerge again in the present century.
That in itself is not surprising. The life of the Church is

woven out of a number of strands, some of which become prominent during one age only to virtually disappear from view in another; but all of them persist under the surface ready to re-emerge when conditions are ripe. There have been times of theological ferment, and times when theology seems virtually to have died. There have been times when the Church has been pulsating with new life pushing out in all directions, and times when it has seemed like a dried husk surviving only because the winds of change have not yet blown it away. And there have been times when the mystical tradition has been a major preoccupation of the Church, times like the fourteenth century in England or the sixteenth century in Spain, and times when the Church seems virtually to have turned its back on mysticism and to have reduced the spiritual life to barren and rigid categories. Today, perhaps, is a time when the current of mysticism is re-emerging.

Chapter Eight

SEEK FIRST THE KINGDOM

All this talk of objections to mysticism and the dangers it can bring with it may seem unnecessarily carping and negative. But the phenomenon of mysticism underlines cruelly the ambivalent and almost schizophrenic situation in which the Christian is placed. On the one hand, we are rooted in this present life. Not only does it provide the categories within which we think (so that anything outside the limitations of space and time in which we live is literally unthinkable unless it can be presented by way of analogy in terms of these categories) but salvation itself is presented in human terms, in the categories that tie us down and limit us ultimately to what can be perceived by this particular human animal, this physical body subject to illness and decay and death and yet with immortal longings that reach beyond the stars. On the other hand, this salvation we are offered is something that transcends these categories and limitations in ways that as yet we cannot understand. As Christians we believe in the resurrection, in the promise of eternal life, yet we cannot say precisely what is involved in this.

Running through the Christian life, then, is a continual tension between present and future, between the here and now and the transcending and transformation of this mundane reality in the life of the kingdom. The danger to which Christianity is always liable is to try to suppress this tension, to concentrate on one pole or the other instead of trying to keep the two in balance. Too much concentration on mysticism can upset the equilibrium, can encourage us to think the kingdom is just around the corner when in fact it is a perpetual "not yet" that one day will be revealed as an eternal "now", with the result that we neglect the duty of living out our Christianity in down-to-earth terms of the hungry and the needy on our doorstep.

Mysticism is a sign that the kingdom of God has come upon us. It is a reminder that, however hard we work to reconcile men and women with each other, however well we learn to respond to the wants of our brother in need, however much we are able to build up justice in this world, it is still not the perfect love and peace and justice of the kingdom. As such it is probably an essential element in the life of the Church, a constant reminder of the pilgrim nature of the people of God that forcibly recalls what the goal of that pilgrimage is.

But it is one element, not the whole thing. That is what perhaps needs most to be stressed about mysticism at the present time when a mood of secular hope may be giving way to a mood of secular despair. At the start of the 1960s, when John F. Kennedy was President, and when within the Church we were still experiencing the refreshing shock of Angelo Roncalli's new and human approach to the exercise of the Petrine office of unity and reconciliation, there was a widespread feeling—perhaps a slightly naive feeling, but hope can be somewhat naive at times—that all would be well and all manner of things would be well in purely human and down-to-earth terms. The political processes could still work for the best, could bring the right men to the top and ensure the adoption of the right policies. There were, true enough, daunting problems facing mankind, problems of development and malnutrition and a totally inequitable distribution of the earth's resources. But they were problems which could and would be solved if tackled with sufficient determination and energy.

Now the whole thing seems to have gone sour. Politically, there has been the dishonor of deeper and deeper involvement in Vietnam, there has been the scandal of Watergate. Here, too, the disillusion has been increased by awareness that over Vietnam many of the crucial wrong decisions were made during the Kennedy presidency, in sharp contradiction to the feeling of hope and renewal experienced at the time. There is no uglier mood than that of those who make heroes for themselves without realizing that all heroes have feet of clay. On a broader front, the world's problems have come to seem increasingly insoluble. The prospect of famine looms nearer, while the population explosion ensures that there will be more mouths to feed.

And the 1960s were the decade that saw the emergence of concern over what urban technological industrial society is doing to our environment, with responsible voices raised to forecast only varieties of doom. That we may already have done our best to make our planet uninhabitable is something none of us likes to think about.

Within the Church, too, the same mood of sourness and despair can be detected. The wild hopes centered on Vatican II have often not been fulfilled. The Church as a bureaucratic institution seems to have reasserted its strength, the Church as a community of love, peace, truth and reconciliation to have become weaker. The pressures of secularization have meant that those who formerly clung to the Church because it expressed their tribal identity are falling away, while many of the younger generation seem repelled by Christianity in its institutional manifestations.

Of course, a prospect of such unrelieved gloom and pessimism must inevitably be a caricature. But the whole point about a caricature is that it emphasizes characteristics already present in the object carica-tured, and if it is a successful caricature its success lies in its bringing to light some aspect of the total truth about a situation or a person that other people recog-nize but have not been able to articulate for them-selves. Equally, it is only when the prospect is gloomy that hope can be seen as a virtue. In other circum-stances it can seem merely the normal response.

At a time, then, when many people are losing faith in their own ability and in the ability of the society to which they belong to control events, when they are tempted increasingly to see themselves as the passive victims of the hammerblows of fate, recourse to mysticism could be a dangerous symptom. It could represent an opting out of the struggle that still needs to be waged on the level of human relationships and human needs. It could, on the other hand, represent a much-needed moment of reflection in order to see more clearly and with fewer illusions what the way forward is on the practical level. Like everything human, it is ambivalent; the extent to which it is positive or negative depends on its context and on the uses to which it is put.

Equally, however, there is a danger if people become so involved in the practical struggle that they begin to confuse the immediate goal, and their own interpretation of what this goal is, with the ultimate and eschatological goal of the kingdom. Here mysticism is needed to restore the balance, to remind us all that what we are trying to achieve can never be achieved within the limitations and categories of this world but must transcend them. And it is only if we aim at the ultimate goal which, in human terms we can never reach, that we stand any chance of succeeding in reaching the nearer and more immediate goals.

Once again, then, it comes down to maintaining the proper balance in our understanding of the Gospel and in trying to live out in our lives what the Gospel is demanding of us. Mysticism contributes to the balance, but it is not on its own the sole criterion of Christianity remaining true to its original mission. The temptation all of us are subject to is to isolate and magnify our own particular realization of what the Gospel is demanding of us here and now, our own individual insights into what it means to be a Christian in our own particular time and place, and turn this into a criterion for judging others. Thus a temptation that has to be (and, as far as I can judge, is being) resisted within the charismatic movement is that of regarding as genuine Christians only those with charismatic gifts, those who have experienced the "baptism" of the Holy Spirit and have known in themselves such peripheral phenomena as speaking in tongues. There is a similar temptation for the Christian activist, that of regarding as genuine Christians only those who are fully committed to and engaged in the struggle for human rights and social justice. There is a temptation for those who are occupied with Church affairs either as full-time professionals or as part-time enthusiasts to regard only those similarly occupied as constituting the Church— which explains some of the short-comings of ecclesiastical bureaucracy. And for the mystic—or rather for the would-be mystic, for the person who is attracted by mysticism without necessarily having any great mystical gifts—there is a temptation of only being willing to take seriously those with similar inclinations.

What this demands of us is tolerance and humility. All of us must have the courage to allow other people to work out their own way to Christ without automatically assuming in advance that it must be the wrong way because it is not our way. All of us must be willing to learn from others how things look from their angle and to use these alien insights to correct the distortions that are naturally inherent in our own limited view. For most of us, inevitably, mystics will be among the others from whom we must learn. The rest of us have too many preoccupations that are perfectly laudable, right and necessary in themselves but prevent us from devoting ourselves wholeheartedly to the mastery of prayer. Nor may we necessarily have those gifts of concentration on God and on the things of God, of being able to lose oneself in contemplating God and what God is doing, upon which the mystic builds. And certainly we lack that obsessive compulsion to know the truth at whatever cost in pain or suffering that drives the mystic towards his lonely goal.

Far from being irrelevant to the rest of us, the mystic is there as a reminder that whenever we think we have got God pinned down, whenever we think we know all the answers and have it all worked out, God has escaped us and is waiting to surprise us. He is a God who is always pulling the rug out from under man's feet whenever man thinks he has found somewhere secure to stand that is not God himself in his infinite unpredictability. He is the God of our future who is leading us on to something we cannot imagine or create for ourselves.

But of this unimaginable future the mystic has been granted a glimpse, a foretaste. To reach this knowledge of God as he is in himself the mystic has to follow a painful and dangerous path. There is the risk that he may uncover within himself fears, anxieties and impulses he cannot control. There is the risk that he may never reach the goal he has set for himself, that he may continually beat up against the cloud of unknowing that separates man from God without ever being able to pierce it. There is the risk of another sort of failure, of becoming satisfied with lesser contentments in a way that can turn the whole thing into a form of emotional self-indulgence.

In this way the mystic sums up in himself, in a particularly acute and sharpened form, the dangers that are involved in any attempt to live as a Christian. Because he is attempting to follow Christ without any hedging or reservations, because he is, as it were, trying to live the Christian life in an absolute form, the dangers are heightened. But even being human is dangerous enough. It means being vulnerable, exposing oneself at every turn to the risk of disappointment, of failure, of hurt, of loss. And being Christian is more dangerous still. It means accepting this vulnerability and always being ready to make oneself yet more vulnerable. Living is a dangerous occupation, and there is no security except in the incomprehensibility of God. And it is that security which the mystic has found.

Notes

Chapter I

1. Eric Gill, *Autobiography*, London, Jonathan Cape, 1940, p. 215.

2. Aldous Huxley, *The Doors of Perception* and *Heaven and Hell*, Harmondsworth, Penguin Books, 1959, pp. 17 and 18.

3. See Ronald Knox, *Enthusiasm*, Oxford, Clarendon Press, 1950, pp. 282-7, for a discussion of Bossuet's at the very least ambiguous attitude towards mysticism.

Chapter III

1. For a brief but useful analysis of this state of affairs, see Michael Oakeshott, *The Voice of Poetry in the Conversation of Mankind*, London, Bowes and Bowes, 1959.

2. See "New Thinking about Prayer," *Herder Correspondence*, May 1969 (vol. 6, no. 5), pp. 133-142, for a discussion of this whole issue.

3. *Tractatus* 6.52, 6.521-2.

4. *Language, Truth and Logic*, London, Gollancz, 1950, pp. 118-9.

Chapter IV

1. John Cassian, *Collationes* x:3.
2. Karl Rahner, "Science as a 'Confession?'," *Theological Investigations*, vol. 3, London, Darton, Longman and Todd, Baltimore, Helicon Press, 1967, pp. 390-1.
3. *Collationes* i:4.
4. ibid i:6.

Chapter V

1. Cassian, *Collationes* ix.31.
2. ibid. x:7.
3. ibid. x:11.
4. *The Cloud of Unknowing*, translated into modern English with an introduction by Clifton Wolters, Harmondsworth, Penguin Books, 1961, ch. 39, p. 99.
5. *The Life of Saint Teresa of Avila by herself*, translated with an introduction by J. M. Cohen, Harmondsworth, Penguin Books, 1957, ch. 11, p. 78.
6. Op. cit. ch. 6, p. 60.
7. *The Ascent of Mount Carmel*, book 1, ch. 1; Complete works, translated and edited by E. Allison Peers, London, Burns, Oates and Washbourne, 1934, vol. 1, p. 18.
8. ibid. book 2, ch. 10-32; ed. cit., vol. 1, pp. 100 sqq.
9. *Confessions*, book 1, ch. 1.
10. Op. cit., ch. 13, p. 93.
11. Op. cit., ch. 25, pp. 175-6.
12. For what Julian has to say about the motherhood of God and Jesus as our mother, see especially chapters 58-63: Julian of Norwich, *Revelations of Divine Love*, translated into modern English and with an introduction by Clifton Wolters, Harmondsworth, Penguin Books, 1966, pp. 164-177.

Chapter VI

1. *The Catholic Review,* Baltimore, Maryland, 18 January 1974.

2. For a good example, see Lothario dei Segni (Pope Innocent III), *On the Misery of the Human Condition,* translated by Margaret Mary Dietz, edited by Donald R. Howard, Indianapolis/New York, The Library of Liberal Arts, Bobbs-Merrill Company Inc., 1969. The introduction provides a useful brief survey of this genre of literature.

3. *Introduction to the Devout Life,* part 1, ch. 13; edited and translated by Allan Ross, London, Burns Oates and Washbourne, 1948, p. 58.

4. *The Cloud of Unknowing,* ch. 5; ed. cit. p. 58.

5. Arnold J. Toynbee, *A Study of History,* London, New York, Toronto, Oxford University Press, 1934, vol. iii, p. 248.

6. For the decisive break Vatican II marked with this oversimplification of the tradition, see Friedrich Wulf, in *Commentary on the Documents of Vatican II,* edited by Herbert Vorgrimler, New York, Herder and Herder, 1967, vol. i, pp. 253-260.

Chapter VII

1. Op. cit., vol. 1, p. 1xv. For the complete text of the Salamanca theologian's defense, see vol. 3, pp. 382 ff.

2. Op. cit. ch. 32, pp. 110-1.

3. Op. cit. ch. 38, p. 118.

4. Op. cit. ch. 5, p. 59.